This book belongs to
_____

This book is dedicated to my children - Mikey, Kobe, and Jojo.

Copyright © 2022 Grow Grit Press LLC. All rights reserved. No part of this book may be reproduced in any form without permission in writing from the publisher. Please send bulk order requests to growgritpress@gmail.com

Paperback ISBN: 978-1-63731-631-3
Hardcover ISBN: 978-1-63731-633-7

Printed and bound in the USA.
NinjaLifeHacks.tv

by Mary Nhin

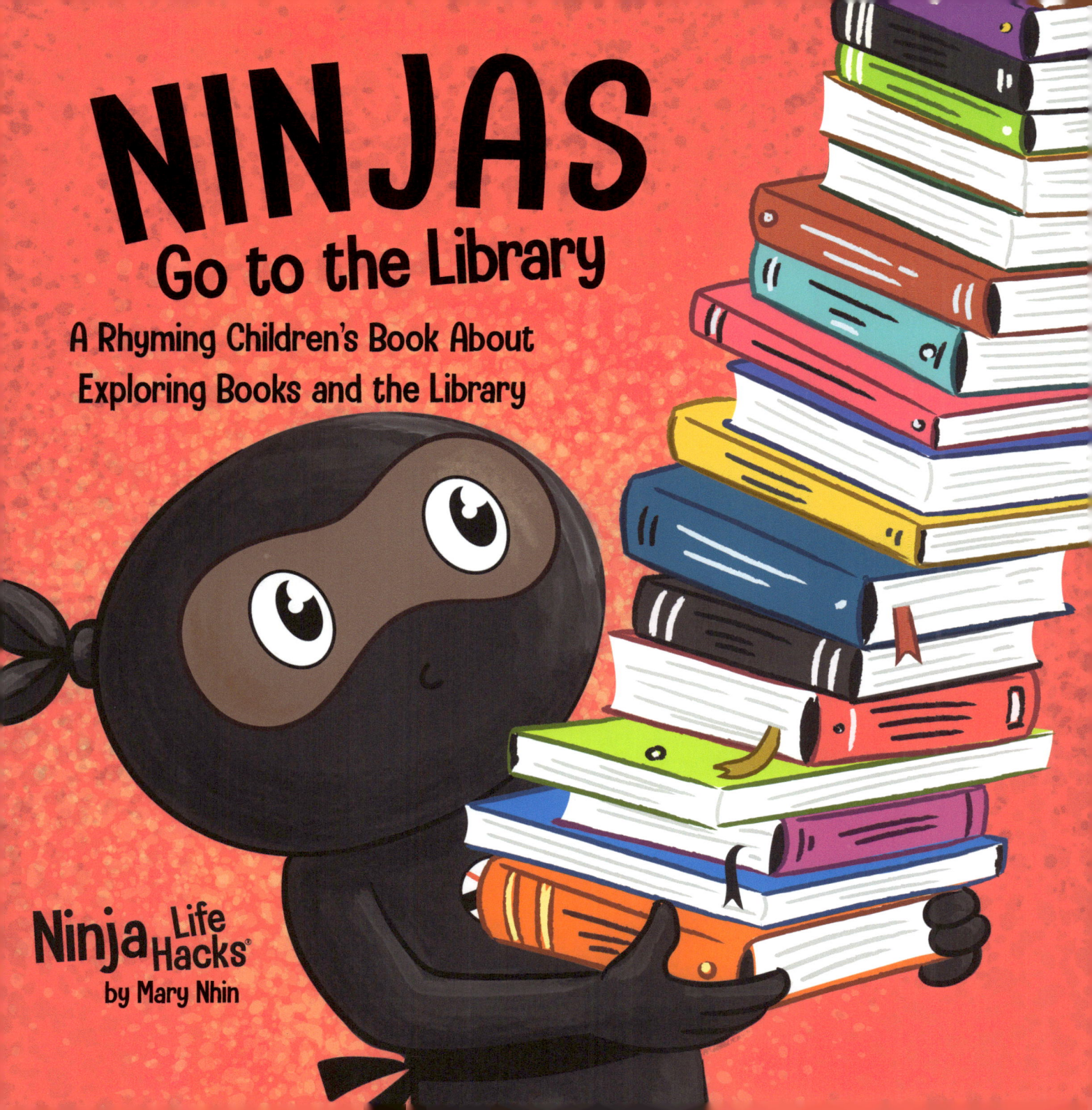

It was the first day of school holiday,
The best time of all to explore.
I set out on an adventure,
To go where I hadn't before.

The playground was crowded and loud,
It seemed every ninja was there.
The beach was the same, the shopping mall too,
As was the ninja town fair.

I walked away from the crowds,
Then, I came to somewhere new.
A magical building with large sliding doors,
And with a deep breath I walked through.

The Library! Wow, what a cool place,
With bookshelves that went for miles!
And so many kids were silently sitting,
Reading books and wearing smiles!

I tiptoed up to a desk,
And asked "Can you help me?
I'd like a book but have no money."
The clerk replied, "Dear, the books are free!"

And for the rest of the school holiday,
I spent my time in there.
Because with a book and your imagination,
You can go anywhere!

I love to hear from my readers. Email me your feedback or thoughts on what my next story should be at info@ninjalifehacks.tv

Yours truly, Mary

 @marynhin  @officialninjalifehacks
#NinjaLifeHacks

 Ninja Life Hacks

 Mary Nhin   Ninja Life Hacks

 @officialninjalifehacks

www.ingramcontent.com/pod-product-compliance
Lightning Source LLC
Chambersburg PA
CBHW041106070526
44583CB00002B/79